Genocide

Issues in Contemporary Civilization

Fascism	Renzo De Felice
Genocide	Irving Louis Horowitz
Socialism	Seymour Martin Lipset
Détente	Aleksandr Solzhenitsyn

TRANSACTION ISSUES

IN CONTEMPORARY CIVILIZATION

Genocide

State Power
and
Mass Murder

Irving Louis Horowitz

Transaction Books
New Brunswick, New Jersey

Library of Congress Catalog Number: 76-2276.
ISBN: 0-87855-191-3 (cloth); 0-87855-620-6 (paper).
Printed in the United States of America.

Library of Congress Cataloging in Publication Data
Horowitz, Irving Louis.
  Genocide: State power and mass murder.
  (Issues in Contemporary Civilization)
  (Social science monographs)   Bibliography: p.
  1. Genocide. I. Title.
JX6731.G4H67   301.5'92   76-2276
ISBN 0-87855-191-3
      0-87855-620-6 pbk

IN MEMORY OF HANNAH ARENDT

If only Cain had chosen words rather than violence, if only he had turned to God and spoken to Him thus:

—Master of the Universe, lend me Your ear. You are my witness as I am Yours. You are my judge and I am afraid, I am afraid to judge. Admit though that I have had every reason to cry out to You my anguish and my wrath; I have every means to oppose my injustice to Yours. Admit that I could strike my brother as You yourself punished my father. Admit that I owe it to myself to protest against the ordeals You impose on man. I could drown mankind with my tears and in its blood. I could bring this farce to an end; that may even be what You want, what You are driving me to. But I shall not do it, do You hear me, Master of the Universe, I shall not do it, I shall not destroy, do You hear me, I shall not kill! Had Cain spoken thus, how different history would have turned out! It would not have been the desperate adventure of two brothers, one of whom asserted himself by killing and the other by letting himself be killed, but the beautiful and passionate, pure and purifying gesture of a noble and fervent mankind.

Elie Wiesel (1976)

Contents

In a cryptic set of marginal notes, Hannah Arendt wrote the following about Horowitz's *Genocide*: "The main question: sociology is the science of society. But is it socially important? ...A sociological analysis of life can reveal no more than the funeral cushions of state power. What you demand can never be found in society, but in law." This brief, but powerful volume comes to grips exactly with these "funeral cushions of state power."

Introduction

Why has sociology failed to achieve the status of a fundamental science—not an important or auxiliary discipline, but a fundamental discipline? In the closing plenary address "Sociologists in a Changing World," delivered before the 1974 meetings of the International Sociological Association, I tried to distinguish between basic and secondary sciences in a forthright manner. I argued that fundamental disciplines involve some aspect of life and death, or, if not death, incarceration and illness. Sociology is denied the status of a fundamental applied science, such as medicine or engineering, because it so rarely comes to grips with issues of life and death. And ordinary people, whatever else may concern them, are moved to seek the advice of others primarily by root considerations. Almost by definition that which is important is related to living and dying; issues of secondary importance are the quality of life and its purpose. Many sociologists exhibit a studied embarrassment about these issues, a feeling that intellectual issues posed in such a manner are melodramatic and unfit

9

for scientific discourse (Horowitz 1975, p. 73). I am not arguing for a theological view of society, or that auxiliary activities are always less important than fundamental activities, but only that the social status of a science in some sense is measured by such easy-to-make but hard-to-prove distinctions.

This study is an effort to give substance to that insight, and in so doing to demonstrate that the underlining predicates of sociology as presently practiced give scant consideration to basic issues of life and death in favor of distinctly derivative issues of social structure and social function. The underlining rationale of this study is a recognition, tragic in its consequences, that the dominant structural-functional categories of explaining the social system increasingly hamper the empirical description of systems by reducing the social order to formal labels or organizational operations. The rise of sociological formalism leads to a presumed isomorphism between societies in theory that is rarely apparent in fact.

The word *fundamental* is itself value laden and extremely troublesome. While there is an able-bodied literature on the moral demand for social science to consider fundamental questions, such as mastery and misery, or producers and products, the dilemma persists that there are so many such general concerns that one is "left with the feeling that the house of social science is still largely founded on sand" (Seeley 1963, pp. 64-65). Another view of the sociologically fundamental is contained in the Millsian distinction between "individual troubles" and "public issues," with those items of national or international historical meaning being highest in the rating chart of the fundamental (Mills 1959, pp. 3-13). But while these are important efforts to establish clear-eyed precepts, they remain ethical strategies and moral postures, rather than sociological efforts to come to grips with the shank of issues.

Life-and-death issues are uniquely fundamental, since they alone serve as a precondition for the examination of all other issues: public and private, local or historical, products and producers (Horowitz 1973, pp. 192-203). Life and death alone moves us beyond a relativistic framework. Those works within social science that have most profoundly gripped our attention over time and through space are linked to problems of life and death. While for the most part our concerns are with life and death as a human, biological fact, we should also consider the life and death of institutions and communities as fundamental social questions (Caudill 1963, pp. 305-324; Cottrell 1951, pp. 356-65). This volume is dedicated to a consideration of genocide in the context of political sociology.

Genocide

1
Defining Genocide

The great contemporary German social philosopher, Ernst Bloch, has aptly written: "We paint images of what lies ahead, and insulate ourselves into what may come after us. But no upward glance can fail to brush against death which makes all things pale" (Bloch 1971, p. 43). Without in any way passing judgment on the strong resistance of some European scholars to current trends in empirical and behavioral sociology (Davis 1975, pp. 389-400), the fact remains that we still do not possess a political sociology that properly encompasses the phenomenon of death. Social psychologists have provided insights into the meaning of death (Becker 1974, 1975) and into its personal consequences (Lifton 1967). But we know precious little about how to account for differences between social systems and state organs that employ mass murder to maintain themselves and those that eschew or resist the ultimate strategy of enforcing the social order by the sacrifice of lives.

We require a large-scale turn away from structures to processes, from systems to humans, not simply to

bring people back into sociology or because of considerations derived largely from humanitarian concerns, but because of basic scientific concerns:
namely, connecting theories employed to explain the
world with what the world itself deems important at
any given time. At this point in sociological time, the
tendency to seek explanations in terms of organization, structure, and system is common to most major
tendencies of sociology, from functionalism to Marx-
ism. Social science at a macro level tends to be satisfied with descriptive statements about trends, stages,
and tendencies. As a result, the measurement bias is
to infer sociological similarities from presumed organizational prerequisites. This very trend weakens
the quantitative aspects of sociological measurement
no less than the qualitative aspects of sociological
theory.

Why employ genocide as a basic mechanism to
overcome the functionalist hubris? The concept of
genocide is empirically ubiquitous and politically
troublesome. Formal definitions are either too broad
to invite action or too narrow to require any; political
definitions invariably mean what *other* nations do to
subject populations, never what one's own does to its
subjects or citizens. Genocide is not simply a sporadic
or random event such as the Katyn Forest Massacre
in which 15,000 Polish troops were presumed to have
been destroyed by the Red Army during World War II
(Zawodny 1962). In addition to its systematic character, genocide must be conducted with the approval of,
if not direct intervention by, the state apparatus.
Genocide is mass destruction of a special sort, one
that reflects some sort of political support base within
a given ruling class or national grouping. This con-

trasts sharply with vigilantism, which respresents the maintenance of order without law, or some kind of mass participation that does not have corresponding state support (Rosenbaum and Sederberg 1976). These are not absolute categories. There is a slim line between systematic and sporadic destruction, and sporadic destruction may take more lives over time than systematic annihilation. Similarly, vigilante politics often has the tacit support of at least a portion of the state mechanism. For example, the vigilante practices of the Ku Klux Klan had the assistance of state houses and court houses in Southern states between 1865 and 1920. Nevertheless, the distinction between genocide and vigilantism is significant and of more than academic consequence. For we are dealing with political structures, not just social events.

The concept of genocide is one of the best defined and least adhered to in the lexicon of modern times. Traditionally, genocide simply meant any attempt to destroy, in whole or in part, any one of a number of various groups. With the founding of the United Nations, the General Assembly, in response to the horrors of World War II, declared in its resolution of 11 December 1946, that genocide "is a crime under international law, contrary to the support and designs of the United Nations, and condemned by the civilized world" (United Nations 1949, pp. 595-99). It received further analysis by the United Nations Economic and Social Council, which appointed a special committee that approved a convention on the subject. This convention was discussed, and finally approved on 9 December 1948 by a unanimous vote of fifty-six to nothing. The crux of the matter is contained in Article Two, which stipulates as follows (United Nations

1950, pp. 959; see also Patterson 1971, pp. 178-79):

> In the present Convention, genocide means any of the following acts committed with intent to destroy, in whole or in part, a national, ethnical, racial, or religious group, as such: (a) Killing members of the group; (b) Causing serious bodily or mental harm to members of the group; (c) Deliberately inflicting on the group conditions of life calculated to bring about its physical destruction in whole or in part; (d) Imposing measures intended to prevent births within the group; (e) Forcibly transferring children of the group to another group.

In addition to this legal definition of genocide, it is necessary to add a sociological dimension. Two points must be subsumed under such a heading: first, genocide represents a systematic effort over time to liquidate a national population, usually a minority; second, it functions as a fundamental political policy to assure conformity and participation by the citizenry. There are exceptions to each point. Sometimes, as it is in the apartheid policy of South Africa, it is the minority that practices forms of genocide on a majority. Also, there are many cases in which overt statements of a government only vaguely reflect its convert actions, for instance, the case of Soviet policy toward its national minorities.

A formal distinction between genocide and assassination is also required. Genocide is herein defined as *a structural and systematic destruction of innocent people by a state bureaucratic apparatus*; whereas assassination is reserved to designate random and sporadic efforts of people without power to illegally seize power and liquidate paramount central figures in a given regime as a means to that goal (Havens,

Leiden, and Schmitt 1970). Assassination, like
genocide, may take the lives of innocent third parties,
but its primary focus is aimed toward the symbolic,
and hence selective, liquidation of powerful enemies.
The distinction between genocide and assassination
is roughly analogous to the difference between force
as the prerogative of state power and violence as the
instrument of those excluded from state power. All
linguistic devices have built-in limitations, and the
fine lines of intellect may be crossed to satisfy the
exigencies of immediate practice. Yet this distinction
between genocide and assassination does permit a
rule-of-thumb separation between death at the hands
of the state, the behemoth; and death at the hands of
the individual, the anarch.

A special type of genocidal practice is employed
against overseas rather than native populations. One
of the fundamental characteristics of nineteenth-
century European imperialism was its systematic destruction of communities outside the "mother country." Decimation of Zulu tribesmen by British troops,
the Dutch-run slave trade, and the virtual depopula-
tion of the Congo by Belgians, typify this form of
colonial genocide. It would be simple to say that such
events are merely a consequence of international
strife and the division of spoils, and that they do not
qualify as genocidal practice. Those engaging in
genocide nearly always define the people to be purged
and liquidated as alien or enemy populations.
Whether they are aliens from within or without is an
ideological caveat that disguises the fact of systematic mass extermination by one state power against a
relatively powerless group or sector. The conduct of
classic colonialism was invariably linked with

genocide. It is the awful heritage of European nations
that they proclaimed concepts of democracy and lib-
erty for their own populations while systematically
destroying others. This was the bequeathal of
nineteenth-century "civilized" existence. This be-
quest of the past became the norm of the twentieth
century.

Although concern for problems of genocide fitted
into the thinking of the United Nations at its incep-
tion, the series of treaties, approved and even rati-
fied, remained largely unenforced. The emergence of
the Cold War, and its attendant polarization of all
conflicts along a communist-anticommunist cost
benefit scale, led to a decline of attention to that very
feature of the twentieth century that presumably
differentiated it from all other centuries: the international protection of the rights of people. And as a
result, the genocidal norm outlasted any organizational efforts to displace it. As Leon Gordenker recently inquired:

> Who made the destruction of the 300,000 or so Indone-
> sian communists after the attempted coup d'état in 1965
> a matter for the United Nations? Who saw the depriva-
> tion of the rights of Asians in Uganda as an outrage?
> Who labelled as genocidal the slaughter of baHutu
> tribesmen—80,000 or so of them—by the waTutsi elite
> of Burundi? How much attention was given to the hor-
> rors of the civil war in Nigeria? Who has tried to ease the
> emergence of Angola by protecting the humanity of all
> involved? Who talks of the operations of the secret polit-
> ical police whose knock at dawn is a common sound in
> dictatorships of the right and left that occupy most of the
> world? Well, not the principal organs of the United
> Nations which for the moment have other priorities in
> the human rights field. (Gordenker 1976, p. 325)

Thus the question of genocide is once again returned to the nation-state. Indeed, if candor is to prevail, statesmen and scholars alike would have to admit that the umbilical cord between genocidal practice and state power has never been stronger.

2
Functional Views of Genocide

A cursory examination of the various forms of totalitarianism reveals weaknesses in the conventional sociological modes of dealing with mass murder.

Defined in strictly organizational terms, fascism is a system in which the state regulates labor and management functions while the bureaucracy grows exponentially with respect to the rest of society, and in which the state apparatus, from education to the military, is harnessed toward insuring its own survival and expansion. State preeminence creates conditions for authoritarian domination over vast populations, national and even international. There are other characteristics of fascist systems. An organizational chart would show that countries such as Italy in 1920-43 and Germany in 1933-45 had considerable similarities: the one-party system, the permanent charismatic ruler, and the mobilization of masses by state-controlled agencies. These are important categories in any discussion of fascism. Yet for those who had to make rational decisions about where to live in the 1930s, Rome in the fascist period was a far less austere and grim place than Berlin in the nazi period.

The difficulty with functional description is best appreciated by taking for granted the correctness of Parsons's analysis of fascism as linked to "the generalized aspects of Western society" stretched to the limit. Included in the Parsonian shopping list of fascist characteristics are: the emergence of an emotional, fanatical mass movement closer to religion than to political movements; huge and sudden shifts in population and demographic patterns; the emergence of nationalization and nationalism; the unwillingness of privileged classes to yield their prestige and power to newer, emerging classes (Parsons 1949, pp. 124-41). While these are certainly elements in fascism, they do not provide a sensitive characterization of fascism as a social system, for they offer meager guideposts distinguishing between fascisms. Functional indicators of fascism are so general that they only serve to describe characteristics of every advanced industrial system. They lack sufficient refinement to permit meaningful distinctions between fascism in Italy, national socialism in Germany, falangism in Spain and elsewhere, or differences between fascist and other social systems (cf. Woolf 1968).

Few events in the annals of twentieth-century genocide equal the treatment of European Jewry by nazi Germany. The dropping of the atomic bomb on Hiroshima might well equal it in horror, but not in sustained magnitude. On 20 January 1942, Hitler's government held a conference in a Berlin suburb, at which time the central administrative authorities of the Third Reich prepared to execute Field Marshall

Hermann Goering's order to "make preparation for the general solution of the Jewish problem within the German sphere of influence in Europe." The total number of Jews slated for extermination was eleven million (Martyrs and Heroes Remembrance Authority 1975, pp. 46-63). The nazi war machine fell short of realizing this number by approximately one-half, since the bulk of Soviet Jewry survived the war, and nations like England and Switzerland were never occupied. Even so, between five and six million Jews were arbitrarily executed between 1939 and 1945 at the hands of the nazis.This figure does not include other groups who also died in concentration camps, such as Poles, Gypsies, and other "undesirables." But treatment of other peoples remained relatively random in contrast to the highly rationalized and total destruction of Jews under nazi occupation. One-third of world Jewry was exterminated during Hitler's rule. The sixteen million Jews of 1939 were reduced to under eleven million by 1945 (Hilberg 1961, pp. 766-67; Dawidowicz 1975).

Rationalization of the nazi program of assassination moved by stages from 1933 declarations that the Jewish problem was uniquely a German curse, the slogan being: "The Jews are our misfortune"; to the 1935-37 period in which the Nuremberg Laws were enacted, decreeing that only persons of German blood or Aryans could be citizens of the German Reich; to the 1938-39 period in which the first concentration camp was opened at Buchenwald and mass anti-Jewish riots occurred in both Berlin and Vienna; and the next step of 1939-40 in which World War II began and ghettos were sealed and converted into concentration camps. Between 1942 and 1944, the bulk of the Jews was exterminated in the many concentration camps that had been developed after the Wansee (Berlin) Conference. It was also during this period that the liquidation of all ghettos throughout Europe was carried out. In the last year of the war, 1945, every attempt was made to obliterate all traces of the various and sundry activities committed in the name of cleansing the Third Reich by destroying the Jewish remnants.

The purpose of reciting these well-known details is to illustrate that the precondition for mass extermination was dehumanization: the conversion of citizens into aliens, first by executive decree, then by legislative enactment, and finally by judicial consent. These legal and sociological events represent the precondition for the execution of genocidal policies by totalitarian states. This progressive delegitimization of minorities was remarkably absent throughout the Stalinist era, although there is no question that Soviet citizens were exterminated by the Soviet system and its secret police. One reason for this differential between communism and fascism is the Leninist persuasion, which argued that anti-Semitism and other forms of national discrimination were capitalist aberrations. Hence, the Soviet regime has always been torn between attacking Jews and other "nationalities" for their "petty bourgeois" manifestations, and attacking anti-Semites and other chauvinists often on the same ideological grounds. Alexandr Solzhenitsyn, in the *Gulag Archipelago*, outlines the high points of the Soviet system of terror, its origins, duration, and structure. Literary devices notwithstanding, one is reminded that we are dealing with the liquidation of roughly twenty million Soviet citizens by the Soviet state.

When people today decry the *abuses of the cult*, they keep getting hung up on those years which are stuck in our throats, '37 and '38. And memory begins to make it seem as though arrests were never made *before or after*, but only in those two years ... the wave of 1937 and 1938 was neither the only one nor even the main one, but only one, perhaps of the three biggest waves which strained the murky, stinking pipes of our prison sewers to bursting.

Before it came the wave of 1929 and 1930, the size of a good River Ob, which drove a mere fifteen million peasants, maybe even more, out into the taiga and the tundra. But peasants are a silent people, without a literary voice, nor do they write complaints or memoirs. No interrogators sweated out the night with them, nor did they bother to draw up formal indictments—it was enough to have a decree from the village soviet .... And *after* it there was the wave of 1944 to 1946, the size of a good Yenisei, when they dumped whole nations down the sewer pipes, not to mention millions and millions of others who (because of us!) had been prisoners of war, or carried off to Germany and subsequently repatriated. (This was Stalin's method of cauterizing the wounds so that scar tissue would form more quickly, and thus the body politic as a whole would not have to rest up, catch its breath, regain its strength.) But in this wave, too, the people were of the simpler kind, and they wrote no memoirs.

But the wave of 1937 swept up and carried off to the Archipelago people of position, people with a Party past, yes, educated people, around whom, were many who had been wounded and remained in the cities ... and what a lot of them had pen in hand! And today they are all writing, speaking, remembering: "Nineteen thirty-seven!". A whole Volga of the people's grief! (Solzhenitsyn 1973, pp. 24-25)

The efforts of Wilhelm Reich to place the Soviet and German experience in cultural perspective are particularly noteworthy. One may argue with his arcane linguistic formulation, but there can be no question of the empirical accuracy of his evaluation:

> The German and Russian State apparatuses grew out of despotism. For this reason the subservient nature of the human character of masses of people in Germany and in Russia was exceptionally pronounced. Thus, in both cases, the revolution led to a new despotism with the certainty of irrational logic. In contrast to the German and Russian State apparatuses, the American State apparatus was formed by groups of people who have evaded European and Asian despotism by fleeing to a virgin territory free of immediate and effective traditions. Only in this way can it be understood that, until the time of this writing, a totalitarian State apparatus was not able to develop in America, whereas in Europe every overthrow of the government carried out under the slogan of freedom inevitably led to despotism. (Reich 1970, p. 281)

To see how ubiquitous the use of labels such as fascism can be, one need only contrast the situation in Germany with that in Italy, both in respect to the general nature of Italian fascism and its particular attitudes toward the Jewish question. In Italy, the Special Tribunal for the Defense of the State was a judicial body created ad hoc by fascism in the Exceptional Laws of 1926, with a view to prosecuting political opponents of the regime and removing them from the jurisdiction of the ordinary magistracy, which had more respect for legality. The Special Tribunal was therefore by its very nature an extralegal judicial body, which often made no effort to give a coher-

ent juridical basis for its sentences or to conceal the
political persecution that was its function. Between
1927 and 1943, the Special Tribunal passed 4,596
sentences for a total of 27,735 years of imprisonment.
Death sentences numbered 42, of which 31 were executed. Those sentenced were members of every social
class and of various parties (cf. Gramsci 1973, pp.
131-32).

In retrospect, the attitude toward Jews seems a
touchstone of fascist systems. While both had similar
forms of political organization, Italy represented an
incarceration society and Germany a genocidal society. The passage of the Racial Laws marked the fundamental rupture between the fascist state and the
Italian bourgeoisie. From 1938 to its collapse in 1943,
the bulk of the Italians, and not simply those in one
class, began to view the regime as something alien to
them. The emergence of official anti-Semitism, restricted though it was to a juridical model, marked
the beginning of the rejection of fascism by large
numbers of Italians and began the period that pro-
duced the eventual downfall of the regime (Chabod
1961, pp. 91-100). It was argued that fascist anti-
Semitism was both unnecessary and extrinsic to the
Italian class system and its cultural components.
Various observers have seen Italian anti-Semitism
as a fundamental component and fatal cause of the
demise of the fascist role in Italy (Ledeen 1973).

This brief description of the relative absence of
mass murder in an incarceration society such as fascist Italy is offered not only to prove that cultural
variables are important components in a social system, but to demonstrate that defining a social and
political system solely in terms of formal characteris-

tics falsifies a comparative analytic framework. To argue the case for a great world historic struggle between facism and communism on the basis of fine ideological distinctions seems less persuasive when we make central the question of officially inspired deaths. On the basis of raw data concerning their official assassination of citizens, nazi Germany and Stalinist Russia are more proximate to each other than either is to Italian fascism or, for that matter, if official murders are a yardstick, to Chinese communism. When we compare the Italian and German experiences with fascism, or the Russian and Chinese experiences with communism, we have the beginnings of a fundamental existential perspective toward social and political life.*

Some fascist or socialist countries can employ virtually no death by state decrees, while in others carrying similar political labels, death may be a commonplace event. This existential dimension of the sociological enterprise must be taken seriously. Whether people live or die is a fundamental distinction that may enable us to make a science of society a fundamental discipline.

---

*Steiner's (1976) serious effort in studying the social psychology of escalation in mass destruction is particularly noteworthy in this connection.

3

Existential Visions of Genocide

It is not my purpose to discuss the entire range of issues related to life and death: deviance, suicide, random assassination, crimes of passion. These are being placed to one side, although they are certainly important; indeed, they are central to any sociological definition of the social system. But here I want to examine a specific problem: the possibility of defining the state not in terms of communism, liberalism, or conservatism, but whether and to what degree it permits the official and arbitrary termination of the lives of its citizenry.

Conventional war will largely be excluded from the purview of this discussion. Deaths occasioned by conflict between states are subject to so many interpretations, such as the right of survival of the state over and above the obligation of individuals to that state, that it is operationally imperative to distinguish warfare from genocide. This decision is further warranted by the weight of current empirical research that indicates that domestic destruction and international warring are separate dimensions of struggle.

"There are no common conditions or causes of domestic and foreign conflict behavior" (Rummel 1969, p. 226). And while this disjunction between domestic and foreign forms of decimation may seem incongruous, even a brief reflection will reveal how often foreign détente permits internal mayhem.

Life-and-death issues have a bearing beyond particular concerns of class or stratification. The subject of the arbitrary termination of life involves a general understanding of the merits and demerits of the social system as a whole. Durkheim well understood this relationship.

> The questions it raises are closely connected with the most serious practical problems of the present time. The abnormal development of suicide and the general unrest of contemporary societies spring from the same causes. The exceptionally high number of voluntary deaths manifests the state of deep disturbance from which civilized societies are suffering, and bears witness to its gravity. It may even be said that this measures it. When these sufferings are expressed by a theorist they may be considered exaggerated and unfaithfully interpreted. But in these statistics of suicide they speak for themselves, allowing no room for personal interpretation. The only possible way, then, to check this current of collective sadness is by at least lessening the collective malady of which it is a sign and result. (Durkheim 1951, p. 391)

I would like to extend this analysis to the area of deaths due to reasons of state. Genocide differs markedly from suicide. Taking one's life, dying for oneself: anomie, altruism, fatalism; or dying voluntarily for one's state in order to uphold the boundaries of a nation; or for that matter to uphold the laws of a

nation, such as in the Socratic death, represents a
phenomenon apart. What we are concerned with is
the arbitrary termination of life against the will of
the individual and on behalf of the collective will of
the state. The burden of these remarks is restricted to
legal murder in which no one is punished other than
the victim; that area of state power that terminates
one life or many on behalf of an abstract political
principle, whether it be national or international in
character.

Hannah Arendt, perhaps the most astute commen-
tator on the subject of genocide, put the matter in
proper perspective when she pointed out that there is
a fundamental difference between totalitarian and
libertarian concepts of law.

> At this point the fundamental difference between the
> totalitarian and all other concepts of law comes to light.
> Totalitarian policy does not replace one set of laws with
> another, does not establish its own *concensus juris*, does
> not create, by one revolution, a new form of legality. Its
> defiance of all, even its own positive laws implies that it
> believes it can do without any *concensus juris* whatever,
> and still not resign itself to the tyrannical state of law-
> lessness, arbitrariness, and fear. It can do without the
> *concensus juris* because it promises to release the ful-
> fillment of law from all action and will of man; and it
> promises justice on earth because it claims to make
> mankind itself the embodiment of the law. (Arendt
> 1966, p. 462)

She goes a good deal further in the idea of a legal
breakdown. Underlining the notion of absence of legality is the idea that the state demands a higher
legality that may be called nature, divinity, or history. The source of authority is no longer human but

transcendental. This fanatic commitment to transcendental notions makes death not only possible, but
thoroughly justifiable as well. What can one do with
those of inferior genetic worth and in opposition to
the best of racial man? Not simply a collapse of law,
but its displacement by a higher law, permits certain
societies to mandate the taking of lives.

> In the interpretation of totalitarianism, all laws have
> become laws of movement. When the nazis talked about
> the law of nature or when the Bolsheviks talk about the
> law of history, neither nature nor history is any longer
> the stabilizing source of authority for the actions of
> mortal men: they are movements in themselves. Under-
> lying the nazis' belief in race laws as the expression of
> the law of nature in man, is Darwin's idea of man as the
> product of a natural development which does not neces-
> sarily stop with the present species of human beings,
> just as under the Bolsheviks' belief in class-struggle as
> the expression of the law of history lies Marx's notion of
> society as the product of a gigantic historical movement
> which races according to its own law of motion to the end
> of historical times when it will abolish itself. (Arendt
> 1966, p. 463)

The social system alone does not explain this drive
to satisfy the requirements of history or nature by
taking the lives of dissidents. Here again, national-
cultural differences between Italians and Germans,
and Chinese and Russians, loom very large. Cultural
traits create their own imperatives: that life is more
(or less) important than death; that rehabilitation is
always (or never) possible; that rehabilitation is val-
ued and supported by money and effort (or a costly
waste of time). The fact that high, genocide societies
cross ideological boundaries like fascism and com-

munism indicates that structural or ideological analysis itself does not exhaust the possibilities of understanding social systems.

There is one shadowy area of genocide that permits the state to take lives by indirection, for example, by virtue of benign neglect, or death due to demographic causes. The kinds of events discussed by Josué de Castro (1952) or Lester R. Brown (1972) cover areas formerly considered as death through natural causes: Malthusian verities of war, famine, floods, plagues, and so on. The efforts of a government to reduce the naturalness of this phenomenon and to harness technology and natural resources to minimize such disasters is itself a central indication of how a society values life. In certain circumstances, specifically in the Soviet Union, the state may be working at cross purposes: performing an active role in the reclamation of virgin soil, hydroelectric dam projects, reforestation, and so on, while at the same time condemning its own citizens to death in police camps, or sometimes even in harnessing manpower in the building of those dams. Thus, too, we must consider the role even of high, genocidal societies in minimizing random death.

Genocidal measurement of the state is to be confined to the area of state power and its attitude toward the sacred or profane nature of the life of its citizenry. As international warfare becomes a decreasing possibility for the settlement of major disputes, and as individuals place greater emphasis on the responsibility of society for their economic or social failures, suicide can also be expected to increase. In this technological vacuum, the fundamental unit for taking or preserving life becomes the state. Measurement of the state's achievements must increasingly be made in terms of demographic mortality factors and the social production of goods in society. The central equation of state achievement is the ratio between the arbitrary consumption of people over and against the necessary production of goods.

Time, too, no less than space, is a crucial element in the characterization of a society as genocidal or pacific. In all social systems, whether in revolutionary or counterrevolutionary causes, moments of great tension lead to a catharsis that often claims many lives. But for a state to earn the appellation of a genocidal society it must conduct the systematic destruction of innocent lives over a finite period of time. Killing must be endemic to the organization of all social life and state activities. On such a scale, one might say that Colombia is close to being the apotheosis of the genocidal society in Latin America, in contrast to such nations as Uruguay and Peru which experience officially sanctioned violence sporadically and even spasmodically, but above all, randomly.

A significant task of the state in establishing a genocidal system is its capacity to politically neutralize vast population sectors. This can be achieved in various ways: through careful news leakages of the physical dangers of resistance; rumors about the number of people subject to destruction; delineation of outsider and insider group distinctions to lessen fears of those not targeted for immediate destruction; and, finally, rewarding portions of the genocidal society for remaining loyal to the state. (Usually, as occurred in nazi Germany, such rewards were simplified by the redistribution of Jewish commerical and business holdings to a sector of the non-Jewish German population.) But whatever techniques are employed, the tacit support or quiescence of the larger population is necessary for genocidal practices to prove successful even in short-run terms. The differential outcome of Jews in nations like Denmark and Poland—in the former they were saved largely through militant support from all social and political sectors, whereas the absence of such broad support in the latter nation markedly contributed to their extermination—would indicate that either tacit support or complete demobilization are prerequisites to the success or failure of the genocidal society.

Finally, a crucial existential distinction should be made between genocide and coercion, between the physical and cultural liquidation of peoples in contrast to mind-bending the will of peoples to a presumed common end. The analysis of genocide does not entail a search for distinctions between good and evil, but, simply and essentially, the discontinuity between genocidal societies and other forms of authoritarian societies that may bear a superficial resemblance. Those who widely practice guilt, shame, imprisonment, torture—those malevolent practices with which so many societies are cursed, but which, nonetheless, do not cross a psychological or for that matter physical threshhold involving the taking of lives—are qualitatively different from genocidal societies.

The argument is often presented that one does not have to go beyond economic explanations to comprehend the nature of genocide. And indeed, as we have seen, the presumed need for economic growth and the very real economic consequences of genocide in redistributing property and goods do play a considerable part in such practices. However, we come upon other examples that compel us to go beyond an eco-

nomic explanation. A particular case in point is the
utilization of the German railroads (the *Reichsbahn*)
in the destruction of European Jewry. The deploy-
ment of railroads for such barbaric ends represented
an "unprecedented event that was a product of mul-
tiple initiatives, as well as lengthy negotiations and
repeated adjustments among separate power structures" (Hilberg 1976, p. 11). The political uses of
railroads was real enough. But more significantly,
the transport of Jews took precedence over the transport of men and materials going to the battle zones;
such human cargo also took priority over industrial
transport. Hence, purely economic uses were super-
ceded by political uses. As a result, the role of the
German railroads in the destruction of the Jews does
indeed open profound questions about the substance
and ramifications of the Nazi Reich.

It is therefore an oversimplification to identify
genocide directly with the developmental process.
Certainly a considerable amount of invariant correlations between the two might occasion such a general theory. However, the number of instances in
which genocidal practices are used to prevent
development—for instance, civilizations that have
employed genocide, especially racial genocide, to
maintain a slave system over and against an industrial system—clearly indicates that something other
than the necessity for industrial growth is operative
as a stimulant to genocide; that something else, that
element which truly distinguishes genocidal societies from industrial societies practicing a wide range
of coercive procedures to maintain patterns of economic growth, is essentially political. When the ruling elites decide that their continuation in power
transcends all other economic and social values, at

that point does the possibility, if not the necessity, for genocide increase qualitatively. For this reason, genocide is a unique strategy for totalitarian regimes. So much so is this the case that even when genocidal practices serve to threaten economic development—as it did in the irrational expulsion and destruction of Jewish scientists from nazi Germany, or the mass incarceration of trained professionals and their reduction to slave labor until the point of death in the Stalinist experience—it manages to take priority over "rational" economic goals. Genocide is always a conscious choice and decision. It is never just an accident of history or a necessity imposed by unseen economic growth requirements. Hence, genocide is always and everywhere an essentially political decision.

The purpose of an authentic political sociology is to provide a theory of the state based on a scale of its preservation and enhancement of life at one end of the continuum, and death caused by the will of the state on the other end. There are all sorts of intermediary stages that complicate our task—for example, forms of suffering such as mass starvation that might make death a welcome relief. Yet genocide as a starting point toward an existential examination of state power seems eminently significant.

4

Toward a New Typology of Social Systems

There are eight types of societies that can be defined on a measurement scale of life and death. I place these eight types of societies within a framework of state power rather than cultural systems. It is not that anthropology was incorrect in its emphasis on the importance of culture, tradition, and language. Without their work the social sciences would be even more bereft of a humane literature than they are at present. The cultural framework has proven unable to move beyond psychological categories of guilt and shame, or to achieve better than a critical radicalism that envision the life and death of systems in terms paralleling the life and death of individuals. The classical tradition in anthropology, at least until the work of people like Eric Wolf, Marshall Sahlins, and Stanley Diamond, among others, was unable to show how state authority, bureaucratic networks, and nationalist claims generated their own forms of genocidal patterns. For the internalization of guilt or shame to be effective there must be a set of external, and usually political, restraints on behavior. Ques-

tions of guilt societies or shame societies not only
entail forms of conservatism and consensus, but also,
as has recently been pointed out, are at the heart of
the revolutionary processes in many newer societies
(Wilson 1974, pp. 253-54).

The following definitions of societal types should be
viewed as guidelines, not as fixed types such as
Spranger's *Types of Men* (1928), but rather as a
continuum. Beyond that, we are faced with the grim
truth that any given nation may exhibit all eight
types of patterns over a sufficient length of time.
Much depends on the primary and secondary definitions of a society rather than the existence of any one
type and the absence of all other types. The types are:

> *First*, genocidal societies in which the state arbi-
> trarily takes the lives of citizens for deviant or
> dissident behavior.
>
> *Second*, deportation or incarceration societies in
> which the state either removes individuals from
> the larger body politic or in some form prevents
> their interaction with the commonwealth in
> general.
>
> *Third*, torture societies in which people are vic-
> timized short of death, returned to the societies
> from which they emanated, and left in these
> societies as living evidence of the high risk of
> deviance or dissidence.
>
> *Fourth*, harassment societies in which deviants are
> constantly being picked up, searched, seized, or
> held in violation of laws that are usually remote
> from the actual crimes the state feels these indi-
> viduals have committed. Since laws can be in-
> voked against almost any behavior, the possibil-
> ity of harassment of individuals through legal
> channels is infinite.

These four types of societies have in common the physical discomfiture and dislocation of deviant, dissident individuals, employing everything from simple harassment for nonpayment of taxes, for example, to direct liquidation of the person. What is involved is physical. There are another four types of social systems that use what might be called the symbolic method for gaining allegiance and adherence. These are:

Fifth, traditional shame societies where participation in the collective will is generated through instilling in the individual a sense of disapproval from outside sources, and insured by the isolation suffered as a result of nonparticipation in the normative system.

Sixth, guilt societies closely akin to shame societies but which internalize a sense of wrongdoing in the individual causing him to respond to normative standards.

Seventh, tolerant societies where norms are well articulated and understood, but where deviance and dissidence are permitted to go unpunished; they are not celebrated, but not destroyed either. These can be described as a series of pluralisms operating within a larger monism.

Eighth, permissive societies in which norms are questioned and community definitions rather than state definition of what constitutes normative behavior emerge in the decision-making process.

These eight types of societies overlap, but they are distinct enough to merit differentiation and understanding on their own terms. Each of these eight types of societies can be found in capitalist, socialist, or any kind of society, whatever its admixture, and it would be futile to claim that the movement from capitalism to socialism requires or involves a movement from less punitive to more permissive, or less permissive to more punitive societies. To attempt such a correlation analysis at this level is a snare and delusion, inviting spurious sorts of measures and correlations.

Capitalism and socialism are, after all, not strictly economic systems. They yield all sorts of mixed political and ideological persuasions. Thus, if we isolate but one item—the number of parties operating in a given social system—we find a similar lack of correlation between types of polity and forms of rule. While it would appear to be the case that single-party states reveal higher levels of coercion than multiparty states, the single-party apparatus of Mexico or Israel (with all due tolerance for the formal existence of smaller, satellitic parties in these two nations) may operate more democratically than the multiparty apparatus in Argentina or Indonesia. In any event, the purpose of this brief study is not to examine the relationship between democratic processes and political parties. Rather it is to develop first a typology and then an explanation for state perpetrated violence that distinguishes genocidal societies from other types of domination and authority.

To Turkey we owe two developments that were to be of profound impact on the course of the twentieth century: at one end there was the Kemalist Revolution that functioned as a prototype for Third World patterns of development a half century later. Both in practice and in concept, Turkey initiated a revolution from above under military bureaucratic sponsorship that took that agrarian society to the threshhold of the twentieth century (Fidel 1969; Trimberger 1976). Equally important, and far more ominous, was the final legacy of the Ottoman Empire. From the start of the century until its final demise in 1918, it bequeathed a policy of genocide on a scale unparalleled in any earlier epoch. The destruction of the Armenians was an event whose magnitude was matched only by the silence of the "civilized world" too absorbed in its own horrors of the First World War to realize the qualitative uniqueness involved in the mass extermination of the Armenian peoples.

> In 1915, the leaders of the Turkish Empire put into action a plan to remove and exterminate its Armenian population of approximately 1,800,000 persons. The Turks were not particular about the methods they employed to this end: of at least a million and a half Armenians forced to leave their homes, supposedly to be deported, from 600,000 to 800,000 were murdered before ever reaching their destinations. Descriptions of this massacre clearly indicate an attempt to deliberately, systematically exterminate all or most of the group. (Dadrian 1971, p. 394)

Even if there remains some slight doubt as to the role of the Young Turks in this genocidal process, there can be no doubt that the drive toward nationalization, ethnic unity, and religious singularity, all contributed to link development and genocidal process in the Kemalist Revolution (Morgenthau 1918; Bryce 1916).

The explanations offered for the genocidal treatment of the Armenians provide crucial elements in any explanation of premeditated mass murder carried out by the state. The summary prepared by Dadrian clearly delineates what these elements are.

(1) Acute interferences with mainly political, military, and economic goal-directed activities gave rise to anger, or aggressive tendencies. (2) The Armenians were perceived as the available source of much of this frustration, and hostile attitudes against them were amplified. The process of scapegoating added to these hostilities angers, which could not be directed toward the actual frustrator, i.e., the opposing Allies. (3) Social and cultural inhibitions which might have directed anger into channels other than aggression were minimal or absent. (4) Hostility became so intense and restraint so weak as to allow aggressive behavior of the most violent nature to occur, thanks to the original decision of the Turkish government to carry out the genocide. (Dadrian 1971, pp. 414-15)

Such basically social-psychological features as external threat, opposing beliefs, competition for scarce goods, and frustration-aggression-scapegoating syndromes are often present in social systems without genocide taking place. These characteristics are often extant during wartime conditions. In this regard Dadrian, himself, has extended his analysis more recently to provide a greater specificity to genocidal systems. In comparing the Armenian and Jewish cases, we are provided with a pioneering typology in the sociological literature.

Primary Importance Common Features
a.   Both acts of genocide were designed and executed during the exigencies of so-called global wars, or world wars.

b. In both instances, the principal instruments for the conception, design, and execution of the holocausts were political parties (Young Turks and Nazis) who invested themselves with monolithic power and literally took over the functions of their respective states.

Secondary Importance Common Features

a. The war ministries, and the selected organs and outfits of the affiliated military structures, were subverted and utilized for the manifold purposes of genocide.
b. Economic considerations involving official as well as some personal designs of enrichment at the expense of the relatively better off members of the victim group, played a key role.
c. In both members, the victim groups were minorities whose overall vulnerability was matched by the degree of ease with which the dominant groups implemented their schemes of extermination.

Tertiary Importance Common Features

a. Cultural and religious, and in a sense racial, differences separated the victim groups from the perpetrator groups—notwithstanding the incidence of certain patterns of assimilation and even amalgamation through which multitudes from both groups were, and felt, identified with one another. Indeed, many Ottoman Armenians and German Jews felt politically and socially, if not culturally, identified with the respective dominant groups.
b. The crucial role of bureaucratic machinery in the administration and supervision of genocidal violence.
c. Sanctions, both negative and positive, were the operationally controlling factor in both cases through which military and civilian personnel, from the

> highest to the lowest echelons of the administrative
> setup, were demoted or promoted, punished or re-
> warded, threatened or cajoled on the basis of their
> attitudes and performances vis-à-vis the processes
> of genocide. (Dadrian 1975, pp. 106-107)

Whether a "symbolic interactionist" perspective really flows from available evidence is somewhat doubtful (Dadrian 1975, pp. 99-120; Dadrian 1974, pp. 123-35). Rather it seems to move the discussion of genocide away from its promising roots in political economy into a softer theoretical plane of social psychology. If anything, the search for metaphor would better take us into the realm of social biology, or more simply, neo-Darwinian survivalist perspec- tives. Metaphorical reasoning, however attractive, still leaves intact a study of the specifics of genocide; more poignantly, how genocide serves as an ultimate test of the stratification of a society and the preven- tion of any realization of equities among different races, religions, tribes, and nationalities. For we must try to demonstrate that genocide is endemic to the social structure, and not simply an aberration within that structure. And genocide must serve as a basic measurement device for creating a new typol- ogy of social and political systems, rather than be viewed as a response to mass contagion or elitist charisma.

As in all high-level generalizations, one must ac- count for sharp variations in political systems. The most extreme of these is a weak state, which under- writes mass violence and human genocide in order to foster its own survival. The most pronounced and unique illustration of this is Colombia throughout the twentieth century. Here we have a nation characterrized by *la violencia* that demonstrates how weak state authority can be yet manage to foster its interests without alleviating mass destruction. The importance of this case is transcendent: the issues of genocidal societies cannot be reduced to a simplistic formula that juxtaposes the anarch with the behemoth, and that presumes that the liquidation of state authority is equivalent to ushering in an age of respect for human rights.

William S. Stokes (1971, pp. 446-69) refers to the Colombian state syndrome as *machetismo*. He notes that Colombia has been in a condition of violence that geographically includes almost the entire country, and worse, the entire century. "When no one caudillo can peacefully subjugate existing opposition, when one or more challengers claim to supreme power, *machetismo* becomes a costly and time consuming methodology for establishing authority. Among seventy nationwide examples of *machetismo* in Colombia in the nineteenth century, one conflict alone took approximately 80,000 lives, and the struggle which covered the years 1899 to 1903 took about 100,000 lives." Colombia is an example of a state that exhibits weak central authority and yet manages, by that very factor, to stabilize a genocidal system.

Since we are concerned with establishing the genocidal social system as a basic category of social life, the Colombian case is just as significant as the Turkish case; and indeed more extended over time. In most cases of recorded genocide, the ruling class, party, or regime establishes itself as supreme and exclusive, but in Colombia an entente took place between two aristocratic, patrician institutions that succeeded in maintaining oligarchic domination even in the twilight of their actual economic power.

Darcy Ribeiro (1971, pp. 295-96) traces such dictatorial state authority during the twentieth century. Assassination societies have in common a "homogenization period" in which real opposition, usually liberal in character, is decimated in a systematic fashion. "Figures based on statistics of recent years show that in 1960 Colombia had a rate of death by homicide of 33.8 per 100,000 inhabitants, whereas that of the United States, by no means a tranquil nation, had 4.5, and Peru 2.2" (Campos, et al. 1964, pp. 407-410). Ribeiro plainly states that the entire social structure came to operate "as the generator of lawless forms of conduct on the individual or the family plane, forms that constitute the regular modes of maintaining the overall regime, or in other words, the very function of the institutions."

> The eruption of violence en masse—with its 300,000 officially admitted murders and surely more than 1,000,000 wounded, exiled, robbed, crippled in one decade—occurs when the overall order represented by the regulative institutions of national scope (government, church, justice, army, police, parties, press) becomes confused with local order in the exacerbation of partisan hatred, everything becoming fused and swallowed up in the same generalized dysfunction. (Ribeiro 1971, p. 296)

Let us take as a third example of a genocidal society a newly emerged nation: specifically Uganda. The following report on differences between Tanzania and Uganda sums up what a genocidal society looks like, when one considers that the estimated eighty to ninety thousand people who have died at the hands of the Amin government represent a considerable slice of the population.

General Amin seized power in an overthrow of the Milton Obote government in 1971. Recently the International Commission of Jurists published a 63-page report of offenses against human rights in Uganda, with some horrifying details of the persecution and murder of individuals and total local communities within this African State. A low estimate is that 50,000 people, who were considered "enemies" of the regime, have been murdered and another 50,000 have been forced into exile. A relative of Amin, who was Ugandan foreign minister from 1971-72 and then sought exile himself, estimated that 80,000-90,000 people have died at the hands of Amin's government. (Carney 1975, p. 434)

The full measure of how a genocidal society operates becomes very clear with such data. Uganda is also a deportation society, having exiled forty thousand Indians within a four-week period of time, and against their will. What is especially noteworthy about viewing Uganda primarily as a genocidal society is that one does not become encumbered with lengthy discussions about communism or fascism, and comparative governments of Europe and Africa. Defining Amin's economic system becomes a secondary intellectual task. Ethnocentricities prevent us from viewing nazi Germany or Stalinist Russia in terms similarly unencumbered by ideological definitions.

One must be careful not to assume that genocide is unique to movements that claim revolutionary outlooks. It is equally the case that reactionary systems can practice genocide on revolutionary movements. The case of Malaysia between 1948 and 1956 is indicative of the extermination not simply of an internal political movement, but of a political movement deemed to represent a national minority, in this case a Chinese minority. In the Malaysian case, the linkage between genocide and ethnocide was apparent. The guerrilla forces never numbered more than 8,000 men, who were eventually defeated by a force of 40,000 British and 45,000 Malaysian home guards. This huge overkill was based on a profoundly erroneous persuasion that the Chinese minority was interested in setting up a Chinese hegemony. As a result, a genocidal policy was followed that took lives estimated to be anywhere from 50,000 to 200,000 people (Fairbairn 1974, pp. 125-74).

One factor remains constant: when industrially advanced societies turn into genocidal states, they tend to maintain high levels of economic productivity; terror produces at least short-run upswings in economic growth rates. This was the case in nazi Germany under Hitler and the Soviet Union under Stalin. When societies are industrially backward, the consequence of high assassination rates is to intensify economic backwardness and/or stagnation. Uganda is a prime example of this latter tendency; the rate of industrial expansion and consumer purchasing power have both fallen off badly since the Amin coup (Schultheis 1975, pp. 3-34).

More recently, attempts have been made to maintain the position of black genocide in America by extending the concept in new directions. Questions have been raised as to whether punitive sterilization, breakdowns in medically advanced obstetrical care, tubal ligations and hysterectomies do not constitute new elements in genocide (Weisbord 1975). The difficulty with assumptions about genocidal characteristics of family planning and medical care is the ubiquitous nature of the data. The steady increase in numbers of black people, even beyond the societal norms as a whole, decreases in occupational differentiations, and crude birth and death statistics (Lerner 1975) would indicate that although the punitive treatment of American blacks continues, such differentials are selective; and, above all, do not have federal sanctions supporting such practices.

The ubiquity of the concept of genocide is nowhere better illustrated than in the treatment of American black citizens by their government. In the antebellum South, the killing of portions of the black population for the purpose of exploiting the remainder represented a systematic policy. Less certain is the designation of genocide as a national rather than sectional policy in pre-Civil War contexts; and even less warranted is the assumption that every form of vigilante behavior in the post-Civil War context represents genocidal policy. Certainly from 1865 through 1945 one could detect a systematic, state-sponsored pattern of legal persecution, economic inequality, and police harassment against black people. Beyond that, health, welfare, and educational differentials have constituted a monumental assault by the white population on the black population (Patterson 1970, pp. 125-32). As late as 1950 these differential policies toward black and white accounted for roughly 32,000 more deaths among blacks than whites, despite the aggregate difference in numbers of black and white citizens. There can be no question that racial discrimination endured by American blacks is unparalleled in American history. What can be questioned is how systematic or structural such practices are at present, in contrast to earlier epochs.

If we are left only with the legal definition of genocide, all manner of problems arise. For example, in speaking of deliberately inflicted measures, or forcible transferring of populations, the question inevi-

tably arises: Who carries out such deliberate and
forcible actions? In the case of the United States,
there seems to be a pattern of vigilantism rather than
genocidal practices by the state for the purposes of
maintaining social order. The range of additional
attitudes by the state toward its black citizens extends from a long line of federal legislation to di-
minished racial animus and racial integration, to an
assumption that legislation simply will not work and
"benign neglect" under such circumstances would be
better than forced integration. This relationship between the United States government and its black
citizens is a complex issue made more so by considerable sectional differences and psychological attitudes. Yet it would be both dangerous and hyper-
bolic to equate the American treatment of its black
citizens with the German nazi treatment of its Jewish
citizens. The demographic information we have concerning crude birthrates and the ever-expanding size
of the black population would move to counter such a
mistaken equation. We are not engaged in active
apologetics for the brutality of hostile white-power
structures toward their black citizens, but this must
nonetheless be distinguished from the sort of systematic extermination associated with the concept of
genocide.

There is a thin line between systematic and
sporadic destruction. Sporadic distruction might take
more lives than systematic annihilation. Vigilante
politics often has the tacit support of at least a portion
of the state mechanism. Nevertheless, the distinctions are significant and of more than academic consequence, for they point to tendencies and trends over
time, and also presume the role of resistance to
genocide among different peoples.

The end of an era when formal declarations of warfare were made also signifies the beginning of a new era in which the line between war and genocide becomes profoundly blurred. The undeclared war in Vietnam, with its mortifying levels of deaths through air attacks, including napalm and jelly bombings and the wide use of chemical defoliants, all of these have made some critics of the war argue that this was a case of genocide (Sartre 1968, pp. 57-85; Bedau 1974, pp. 5-46). Arguments were made on the other side that the Vietnam conflict was not a matter of genocide, since the killings were not systematic, but simply a result of the enemy not accepting the terms of an honorable settlement. The distinction between internal peoples and foreign peoples who are being killed helps little, since it must be confessed that all genocidal practices involve a definition by the perpetrators of mass violence of those destroyed as outsiders. What legitimately can be asserted in such cases is that the widespread use of mass violence by state authorities against one portion of a population clearly has spill-over potentials for another part of humanity; sometimes thousands of miles away. This in itself might serve as a deterrent to any further legitimation of a genocidal state.

Peoples subject to genocide have been faced with their strategic requirements for negotiating their own survival. Black resistance to lynchings, hangings, and vigilantism in general served as a major obstacle to genocidal policies, just like in the antebellum South the totality of intimidation weakened such resistance by limiting the social organization of the black community. The literature on the holocaust is filled with similar choices and decisions. The Warsaw Ghetto is perhaps the classical model of Jewish acquiescence being replaced by Jewish resistance once the choices were starkly narrowed to life-and-death concerns. But clearly, whereas in the case of the American black community its struggle for survival was potentially victorious, the same was not the case in the liquidation of the European Jewish communities under nazism. There is no a priori assurance that either acquiscence or resistance will guarantee survival within the confines of a genocidal regime. This is a constant problem that must be faced not only for those aiming at the death of the minority population but for those negotiating the survival of that population as well. In this regard, the definition of the genocidal enemy as external, as was done in the Vietnam conflict, may assist in the liberation effort.

A major category left unresolved by our model is the function of genocide due to imperial aggression or foreign intervention. Here we have the contradiction of fine, upstanding European and American cultures being responsible for the liquidation of masses of native populations. There is the destruction of the Zulu peoples by the British; the decimation and virtual elimination of the Indians by early American settlers; and the impoverishment of the Zaïre peoples in the former Belgian Congo. These are forms of genocide against foreign peoples rather than nationals. A central tendency in all genocidal societies is to initially create juridical-legal separations between citizens and aliens, elites and masses, dominant and backward races, and so forth. This serves as a pretext for genocide and also as a precondition to the implementation of genocidal policies. We are dealing with an oblique problem that has many ramifications: attempting definitions of social systems, not on economic grounds alone, nor any of the other customary variables of polity, military, and society, but rather on mortality data. American Indians and African Zulus, many of whom sought pacific solutions, were defiled and denied even the remote participation of their numbers in any dominant imperial framework. Again, we have the seeds of a study unto itself. Yet the role of classical imperialism as a critical element in creating the conditions for modern mass genocide cannot be ignored.

Although I wish to dedicate at least some brief space to the other seven types of systems that can be measured in terms of a life/death measurement scale, quantitative indicators should not blot out the considerable differences that exist between genocidal societies and all other types of social systems, even the most proximate: deportation-incarceration; torture; and harassment societies. One can recover from torture; one can come out of prison; one can return to a native land; and one can endure harassment even of a systematic variety. But from death there is no return. Not even the quaint Soviet ideology, which permits "posthumous rehabilitation," is really more than a bizarre recognition of the ultimacy of the arbitrary termination of life in the service of state power. The brevity with which I treat the seven remaining types of social organisms is not indicative of their unimportance, nor meant as a relative weighting of how many such societies there are, but represents an effort to retain the essential focus of this book.

A good illustration of the deportation-incarceration society is found in Cuba following the Castro revolution. Without minimizing the enormity of its social reformation, the fact remains that approximately one million Cubans were sent or went voluntarily into exile, out of a total population of less than eight million. One can argue that deportation is an incredibly humane form of treatment compared to assassination, and that, of course, is absolutely true. It is also more humane to use incarceration than incineration, although of the latter Cuba had its share as well. The point is not humanity but forms of punishment, and how the state removes deviants and dissidents from its midst. It is exceedingly important to emphasize the difference between assassination and incarceration societies. It is the most fundamental distinction of all since those either deported or incarcerated usually live to tell the story. This is not to deny that deportation and incarceration are fundamental methods of dealing with and eliminating enemies of the state.

Easier to recognize as a pure deportation society than Cuba, is France and its political police under Napoleon III in the mid-nineteenth century. After the coup d'état of 1851, Louis Bonaparte inaugurated a system of dictatorship that entailed illegal acts. With respect to deviants, criminals, and dangerous political elements, no differentiation was made. A "mixed commission" comprised of civil and military authorities passed sentence without concern for evidence, procedure, or appeal. The convicted would be deported to Guiana or Lambessa. In nineteenth-century terms, the numbers were impressive. By the middle of March 1842, over 26,000 persons had been arrested, of whom six thousand five hundred were acquitted and somewhat more than five thousand sentenced only to police surveillance. Of the fifteen thousand actually punished, nearly two-thirds were sentenced to deportation to Algeria, while the rest were either handed over to other tribunals *against* common law or expelled from France (Bramstedt 1945, p. 39). Despite the severity of punishment, expulsion was viewed as the ultimate punishment rather than the outright elimination of "undesirable elements."

Some societies, like contemporary Brazil, have no capacity to remove or deport enemies of the state. They thus become high, torture societies where police and other agencies of the state minimize opposition and maximize obedience through human disfigurement (Della Cava 1975, pp. 623-26). The numbers tortured are of course important. In countries like Brazil or present-day Chile the numbers reach into the tens of thousands. One must once again distinguish torture both from assassination or incarceration. For the most part, those tortured quickly return to the larger society. One might argue that the purpose of a torture society is to reinfiltrate these people into the larger society as a mechanism of contagion and mass fear.

When referring to Brazil as a torture society, I specifically have in mind the treatment by state authorities of its urban white citizenry. Like the nineteenth-century United States in relation to its Indian minorities, the twentieth-century Brazilian state in relation to its Indian minorities has adopted entirely genocidal standards.

The huge losses sustained by the Indian tribes in this tragic decade were catalogued. Of 19,000 Munducurus believed to have existed in the thirties, only 1,200 were left. The strength of the Guaranis had been reduced from 5,000 to 300. There were 400 Carajas left out of 4,000. Of the Cintas Largas, who had been attacked from the air and driven into the mountains, possibly 500 had survived out of 10,000. The proud and noble nation of the Kadiweus—the Indian Cavaliers—had shrunk to a pitiful scrounging band of about 200. A few hundred only remained of the formidable Chavantes, who prowled in the background of Peter Fleming's Brazilian journey, but they had been reduced to mission fodder—the same melancholy fate that had overtaken the Bororos, who helped to change Levi Strauss's views on the nature of human evolution. Many tribes were now represented by a single family, a few by one or two individuals. Some, like the Tapaiunas—in this case from a gift of sugar laced with arsenic—had disappeared altogether. It is estimated that between 50,000 and 100,000 Indians survive today. Brazil's leading social historian believes that not a single one will be alive by 1980. (Lewis 1974, pp. 9-10)

There are harassment societies where those in opposition to the state are not physically mistreated so much as legally abused. The range of societies performing such harassment extends from large states like the United States to much smaller societies in Western Europe that likewise engage in mass forms of harassment to guarantee political allegiance. Here the purpose is to harness the legal mechanism to the aims of the state so that all forms of harassment appear to be for real crimes rather than political crimes, and hence punishment becomes a nonpolitical response to political opposition.

The fundamental characteristic of the shame society is the idea of rehabilitation: errors against the state are responded to by making the individual criminal feel a sense of shame, and hence the need for reformation. China comes to mind as the best example of that kind of system. Both military and civilian authorities are oriented toward the aim that everyone can be rehabilitated; and this rehabilitation is best defined by self-recognition (shame) and the internalization of guilt. In actual practice, the gulf between shame and guilt societies may be quite narrow.

Vigilante groups are a powerful deterrent to crime. Militia patrols tend to deal out rough justice to offenders on the spot instead of bringing them before civil authorities. This usually takes the form of a beating for crimes of theft or pilfering. The militia is also expected to take part in propaganda work and to change the thinking of bad elements. A recent (official) report from Tientsin talked of militia units "organizing, arming, and propagandizing the masses and rebuffing the wrecking activities of a handful of class enemies." The People's Militia appears to do quite an effective job of law-and-order maintenance. Its main drawback is that a paramilitary organization of this sort can sometimes grow too powerful.

> The first task of the militia is to back up the People's Liberation Army in time of war. Urban units in large cities are trained in sophisticated techniques of warfare, including antiaircraft defense, rocketry, antitank exercises, and tunnel warfare. The second function of the militia, however, is to assist the public security forces in maintaining law and order, and militiamen and women on patrol with rifles and fixed bayonets are a familiar sight. (Jones and Ruge 1975, pp. 20-21)

Guilt societies are less concerned with psychological manifestations than with the sociological recognition of wrongdoing. The guilt society rests on the clear recognition that there is such a thing as deviance from norms, and that those who perform deviant acts are guilty by virtue of that fact alone, and those who are normative are innocent by virtue of obedience to those norms. Guilt societies rest on the justification of normative behavior, and on the assumption of deviants as well as punishers of the soundness of the social order.

Perhaps the classic model of the tolerant society is Great Britain, where norms, rituals, and rites are fully understood and appreciated, but minority views are also found in great abundance. What characterizes these societies is firm allegiance to normative behavior and nondeviant behavior, while the normal apparatus of the state remains nonpunitive. It is left to the citizenry to apply proper social pressure to obtain obedience to the law. In the tolerant society the practice of intimidation is carried on informally rather than formally: normatively rather than legally.

Finally, there are the permissive societies. They are identified by their open-ended response to the question of what constitutes moral law or normative behavior. The permissive society not only tolerates deviance and dissidence, but also understands that the role of the state is nothing other than the orchestration of a series of dissident and deviant acts without appreciation or understanding of what constitutes the perfect norm. Every permissive society has its legal limits, but even these tend to be stretched on behalf of the perpetrator no less than the victims of crimes, so that the legal system is involved in a series of plea bargains. They are not only presumed innocent, but also guilt is relatively shared by all concerned in the criminal process.

Where the United States might fit in such a modeling device is a subject for an entire volume. The brief discussion on its treatment of black people indicates similitudes and continuities with nations elsewhere.

Yet there is a special feature: the United States illus-
trates all eight elements in this typology; from the
conduct of genocide toward its black population in the
nineteenth century to permissive liberalism toward a
variety of interest groups and deviant forces in the
late twentieth century. One might argue that any
typology that cannot adequately settle accounts for
the United States (and as we have already noted,
countries like Brazil) is not worth much; that we are
better off utilizing old-fashioned categories such as
capitalism and democracy. I think not. Such a typology as has herein been presented provides a new basis
for the comparison of the United States with other
societies. True enough, to be left with an eight-part
modeling device as an explanation of the United
States raises proper questions as to the generalizabil-
ity of the model. On the other hand, the mix between
these eight items becomes crucial in the case of Western democratic states. Beyond that, the very inability
to place the United States, or similar such nations,
such as Brazil, in any one (or two) frames of the model
itself indicates the complexities of advanced nations;
not a need to return to an oversimplified model based
on entirely mechanistic variables. The issue of the
United States and other Western liberal societies can
better be resolved once some clear-cut measures are
established for those other countries, and they are in
the disastrous majority, which reveal strong tendencies to fit into one or another of these frames.

The problem of applying the model to concrete
cases notwithstanding, we at least have a first sketch
of eight types of societies (by no means separated into
airtight compartments) in terms of a life/death continuum. Almost every society, and not just the United
States, has all eight types present in one admixture

or another. It becomes the next analytic task to de-
termine the essential characterization of the system
and the point where quantity is transformed into
quality: at what point the numbers of people involved
in sanctions by the state begins to define the character of that state.

Beyond an appreciation of the types of societies
that promote or oppose genocidal practices is the final
realization that "types" of people are extremely resis-
tant to their own elimination. The black population of
the United States is larger in numbers and percen-
tages than at any time in its two-hundred-year history. Despite the utter and near-total decimation of
European Jewry at the hands of the Third Reich, the
total present-day Jewish population is equal to, if not
greater than, at the start of the Second World War.
Even the American Indian population of the United
States has doubled between the census reports issued
in 1960 and again in 1970. Without becoming self-
satisfied or counseling benign neglect about the problem of genocide, it is nonetheless a fact that resistance to destruction of one's group or person should
not be minimized; even in this age of maximum state
power.

5

Personal Life and Social Structure

We must return to the primary distinction between genocidal societies and other types, even those most identified with incarceration. The distinction between societies that do and do not take the lives of people on behalf of state power is the *fundamental* distinction in the twentieth century.

Quite beyond the distinction between life and death, viewing social structures in basic terms may prompt a better understanding of why some societies generate single-party machineries, powerful secret police, and a war apparatus dedicated to geographic expansion, while others do not. We may hypothesize that the higher the level of repression within a society, the greater the need for an apparatus capable of exercising maximum control. Genocidal societies, therefore, usually have either single-party or an absence of party machineries. They also reveal a striking similarity between those who have political power and those who exercise administrative and bureaucratic power. Finally, they display a police apparatus far larger than that required to simply maintain a control of order. These mechanisms aimed at insuring obedience, are themselves exceedingly costly. They represent a chink in the armor of the genocidal society, a weakness that creates the need for greater repression at higher costs, while at the same time the potential and even necessity for more manifest resistance. It might well be that the cost factors of genocidal-assassination society are so exorbitant in economic terms no less than human terms that those in charge of governments are likely to think most carefully about going that route.

A further theoretical possibility is to develop relationships between insiders and outsiders in assassination and permissive societies. The more complete the assassination society, the more firm the distinction of who belongs and who does not, between those who are human and those who are not. The higher the degree of tolerance, the less important is the distinction between belonging and nonbelonging, insiders and outsiders. When one considers the difference between the Jews of Italy and the Jews of Germany, it becomes painfully apparent that Italian Jews were always known as Italians, and their Jewishness was marginal, hardly understandable to most Italians. For the Germans, the difference between being a German and being a Jew was the paramount distinction at every level: biological, demographic, historical, and all the rest. The society became dedicated to making that distinction, for once made, genocide became easy, even normative. Intense nationalism, in contrast to cosmopolitanism, is itself an essential characteristic of the genocidal society. It instills not only a sense of difference between those who belong and those who do not, but also the inhumanity of those who do not belong, and thereby the rights of the social order to purge itself of alien influence.

Just how important the differences are between genocidal and nongenocidal societies, and certainly between punitive and permissive societies, is indicated by nations like Turkey and Japan that, almost without parallel, developed revolutions from above far in advance of other nations in the Third World. The cultural component, the belief in the military ethic, permitted the development of elites to mobilize the society toward developmental goals. Unconstrained by democratic norms, these societies were in a position to set the model for Third World development between fifty and one hundred years earlier.

In his brilliant book *Society and Democracy in Germany*, Ralf Dahrendorf offers a new beginning to solving old problems about the nature of equity. Democracy extends from "equal citizenship rights having to be generalized, to conflicts being recognized and regulated rationally, elites reflecting the color and diversity of social interests, and public virtues as the predominant value orientation of the people." He goes on to say that, strictly speaking, we need a theory of human relations as well as organizational frameworks. As a precondition for a theory of democracy and social structure we need a theory of attitudes toward life and social structure. What can democracy ultimately mean except respect for the lives of people and recognition that one life is as valuable as another? Life itself is a precondition for the democratic social order. It was the breakdown of this sensibility during the nazi period, and the inculcation of what Durkheim refers to as "the myth of the state," that ultimately made impossible the practice of democracy in a world with German nazism. Dahrendorf refers to this peculiar megalomania as a suspension of civil liberties in order to fulfill the imaginary requirements of historical retribution.

Such metaphysical predispositions to correct the con-
tours of history lead not just to government with
authority, but also to an idea of the state as ultimate,
irreversible, and untrammeled by individual ideas.
Whether it is a matter of German character, German
militarization, or German ethics becomes less important than the fact that the society conducted itself in
such a way as to violate any notion of a theory of
democracy (Dahrendorf 1967, pp. 205-209).

The democratic societies of the United States,
Great Britain, Italy, France, Japan, and so on, have
as many differences as similitudes. If we were to take
systems that have been characterized in some period
of their history as fascistic, such as Italy, Germany,
and Spain, we would have at least as many differences as similarities. In the present period, even the
socialists from the Soviet Union to China, and from
the East European nations to Cuba, have as many
differences as similarities. That is why the analysis of
social structure in terms of the formal organization of
society may be a necessary condition for explaining
the system, but it is not a sufficient condition for
explaining the society as a whole.

The point of these remarks is not to displace political or military factors: that would be a game of model
building. My interest is not to superimpose culturol-
ogy upon sociology. I am not suggesting that trans-
historical concepts of spirit be substituted for his-
toricity of all things. A cultural science would
trivialize social science and return us to a condition of
Kulturwissenschaft of Dilthey and Rickert. It has
taken nearly a century to extricate ourselves from
this cultural standpoint, and by no means would it be
worthwhile to return to it. Cultural values, like economic interests of political systems themselves, all

have a common denominator, and that is the attitude toward life within a society, and what the state does to a life, or a series of lives, to foster its own general interests. In that way the series of determinisms that plague social science can be reduced to a general theory of society: one that takes seriously not so much cultural phenomena in contrast to economic phenomena, but the obligation of both to deal seriously with facts of life and death.

We are in the midst of an enormous emotional as well as intellectual upheaval. It extends from questioning the biological meaning of life to the political taking of life. Normative and empirical standards are both being entirely overhauled. Even the most humane are now touched by the matter-of-factness of dying. A clinical view of death is a prelude to a cynical view of the tasks of social systems. In this way, the notion of a political community based on the need to live is being replaced by a vision of pluralism that is nothing more than separated, isolated interest groups tearing at each other's flesh; or at the other end of the political spectrum, demands for authority and order that eat away with equal vigor at the practice of democracy.

To presume obligations to the state is not to assert simply a theory of obedience, but rather that the state must insure the right to live without presuming the reasons for living. The management of a society may extend to commands for obedience based on the need for mutual survival, but not beyond that point. Negotiating the rights of individuals and what one does with a life, is not a matter of state power. Too much normative theorizing is subterfuge for reintroducing a doctrine of individual obligations in place of political rights. The record of the twentieth century

is soiled by a juridical standpoint that asserts obligations to serve the state without any corresponding
sense of the right to life within a state. Michael
Walzer speaks quite directly to this point: "It is surely
not the case that being and feeling obligated are the
same. It is not enough that a common life be felt or
thought to exist; there must *be* a common life. I do not
mean to defend all those nationalistic or ideological
mystifications that lead men to believe they are living in a community when in fact they are not"
(Walzer 1970, p. 98).

One cannot conclude such an examination without
at least a brief inquiry into the nature of responsibility for acts of genocide. The efforts of Richard A. Falk
are significant in this connection. Recognizing
genocide as the most extreme offense of governments
against humankind, he distinguishes between two
types of models for its legal punishment: first, the
indictment model "based on the plausibility of indictment and prosecution of individual perpetrators
before a duly constituted court of law operating ac-
cording to due process and adhering to strict rules of
evidence." Second, he offers a responsibility model
that is based on the community's obligation to re-
pudiate certain forms of government behavior and
the consequent responsibility of individuals and
groups to resist politics involving this behavior"
(Falk 1974, p. 126). While this distinction is salient, a
dilemma of this legal formula is that the genocidal
state is the least likely to permit such neat distinctions from being carried into practice. As Falk himself is sadly compelled to admit: "It must be acknowl-
edged, finally, that individual acts of conscience and
of resistance may be virtually impossible in a ruth-
less and efficient totalitarian system" (Falk 1974, p.
136). Thus, any efforts to move beyond genocide must

again be thrown back upon the political arena, since the relief sought in international law is likely to prove chimeric.

My concern is the establishment of an authentic "sociobiology," one that is grounded in the polity rather than zoology: the social world of the political system in terms of lives taken, years removed from individuals through imprisonment, damages to people through fear of speaking freely. We have moved much too far toward expanding the banality of evil as a necessary component of state existence. One can only hope that such a view of the social order will provide a methodological device for the measurement of social systems, a measurement equal in quantitative power to money for economic science. Quite beyond the methodological aspect is the ideological sense that life is not only worth living, but also that the very task of the social scientist should largely be taken up with an exploration of how to expand such worthiness in life.

One might well inquire as to the feasibility of ever understanding genocide at the empirical level, for example, whether it would not prove more efficacious to search out those aspects of state power and social order that promote equity and well-being rather than leap to ultimate conclusions and terminations. Such an alternative approach is possible. In my typology I indicate forms of permissive and open-ended state bureaucratic behavior that discourage genocidal outcomes. Yet one is left with the strong feeling that a wider appreciation of state authority in its efforts to preserve the social order lead to a conclusion not unlike that reached by eighteenth-century utilitarians and nineteenth-century libertarians alike: that the government governs best that governs least. Instead of inventing a new radius of state activities labeled "social welfare," social scientists might well turn their attention to more fundamental issues of the optimum size for sound governance, or how much economic "waste" is worth what sorts of social "values." I am not suggesting that meliorative issues be abandoned by social research, only that basic issues of life and death not be overlooked in the process.

What conclusions can be drawn from this study? It would be superficial to say that we should bend every effort to expose and prevent any and all forms of genocide. This reflects a rather obvious and basic humanitarian persuasion, one that hardly would be defeated or voted against. Nations that have systematically practiced genocide are not only sponsors of United Nations resolutions against genocide, but have also often urged the strengthening of such resolutions, such as the Soviet desire to add to the genocide resolution a concept of any deliberate act having to do with destroying various cultural, racial, or religious beliefs. The very fact that such resolutions can be introduced by a nation that in the past has widely practiced genocide would indicate that something other than polemics is called for.

What can and should be concluded intellectually is that given the widespread practice of genocide and its virtual autonomy from both economic systems and geographical locations, one should be extremely cautious about the potential for good works of any nation-state. So much fanaticism and rampant chauvinism is generated by mindless adherence to national goals that the use of genocide as a righteous instrument of national and state policy has become highly tempting. Genocide as a technique for achieving national solidarity takes various forms as we have seen. In the United States, with respect to the

Indian question, it is the absorption of "backward tribal nations" into the general nation. In the Soviet Union it has been the liquidation of bourgeois nations into a general socialist commonweal. In short, genocide is a fundamental mechanism for the unification of the national state. That is why it is so widely practiced in "advanced" and "civilized" areas, and why it is so incredibly difficult to eradicate.

The need for faith, trust, and transcendence can be presumed constant. However, it would be dangerous counsel to assume that nations can properly contain and channel such psychic dispositions. It would be wiser to urge faith in Providence, and trust in people. As for transcendence, an appreciation of the immanence of all existence and the transience of all nations might keep in check those proclivities of the powerful to bend, mutilate, and destroy innocent sections of the human race in order to safeguard a world of order without compassion, and ultimately of law without justice.

References

Arendt, Hannah. 1966. *The Origins of Totalitarianism*. New edition. New York: Harcourt, Brace, and World.

Becker, Ernest. 1974. *The Denial of Death*. New York: The Free Press-Macmillan.

———. 1975. *Escape from Evil*. New York: The Free Press-Macmillan.

Bedau, Hugo Adam. 1974. "Genocide in Vietnam?" In *Philosophy, Morality, and International Affairs*. Edited by Virginia Held, Sidney Morgenbesser, and Thomas Nagel. New York: Oxford University Press.

Bloch, Ernst. 1971. *Man on His Own*. New York: Herder and Herder.

Bramstedt, E. K. 1945. *Dictatorship and Political Police: The Technique of Control by Fear*. London: Kegan Paul, Trench, Trubner and Company Ltd.

Brown, Lester R. 1972. *World Without Borders*. New York: Random House.

Bryce, James. 1916. *The Treatment of the Armenians in the Ottomon Empire*. London: Macmillan Ltd.

Campos, German Guzmán; Borda, Orlando Fals; and Luna, Eduardo Umaña. N.d. *La Violencia en Colombia: Estudio de un Proceso Social*. Bogota.

Carney, Martin. 1975. "Amin's Uganda." *The Nation*, 12 April, pp. 430-35.

Caudill, Harry M. 1963. *Night Comes to the Cumberlands: A Biography of a Depressed Area*. Boston: Little, Brown. An Atlantic Monthly Press Book.

Chabod, Federico. 1961. *L'Italia Contemporanea, 1918-1948*. Torino.

Cottrell, W. F. 1951. "Death by Dieselization: A Case Study in the Reaction to Technological Change." *American Sociological Review* 16, no. 3 (June):358-65.

Dadrian, Vahakn N. 1971. "Factors of Anger and Aggression in Genocide." *Journal of Human Relations* 19, no. 3:394-417.

———. 1974. "The Structural-Functional Components of Genocide." In *Victimology*. Edited by Israel Drapkin and Emilio Viano. Lexington, Mass.: Lexington Books-D. C. Heath.

———. 1975. "The Common Features of the Armenian and Jewish Cases of Genocide: A Comparative Victomological Perspective." In *Victimology: A New Focus: Violence and Its Victims*. Edited by Israel Drapkin and Emilio Viano. Lexington, Mass.:Lexington Books-D. C. Heath.

Dahrendorf, Ralf. 1967. *Society and Democracy in Germany*. Garden City, New York: Doubleday.

Davis, Devra Lee. 1975. "Theodor W. Adorno: Theoretician Through Negation." *Theory and Society* 2, no. 4:389-400.

Dawidowicz, Lucy S. 1975. *The War Against the Jews*. New York: Holt, Rinehart, and Winston.

de Castro, Josué. 1952. *The Geography of Hunger*. Boston: Little, Brown.

Deker, Nikolai, and Lebed, Andrei, eds. 1958. *Genocide in the U.S.S.R.: Studies in Group Destruction*. New York: The Scarecrow Press. (First published in Germany by The Institute for the Study of the U.S.S.R.)

Della Cava, Ralph. 1975. "Brazil: The Struggle for Human Rights." *Commonweal* 102, no. 20:623-26.

Durkheim, Emile. 1951. *Suicide: A Study in Sociology*. New York: The Free Press-Macmillan.

Fairbairn, Geoffrey. 1974. *Revolutionary Guerrilla Warfare: The Countryside Version*. Harmondsworth, Middlesex: Penguin Books Ltd.

Falk, Richard A. 1974. "Ecocide, Genocide, and the Nuremberg Tradition of Individual Responsibility." In *Philosophy, Morality, and International Affairs*. Edited by Virginia Held, Sidney Morgenbesser, and Thomas Nagel, pp. 123-37. New York: Oxford University Press.

Fidel, Kenneth. 1969. *Social Structure and Military Intervention: The 1960 Turkish Revolution*. Ph.D. dissertation, Washington University, St. Louis.

———. 1975. "Military Organization and Conspiracy in Turkey." *Militarism in Developing Countries*. Edited by Kenneth

Fidel, pp. 169-218. New Brunswick, N.J.: Transaction Books.

Gordenker, Leon. 1976. "Symbols and Substance in the United Nations." *New Society* 35, no. 697 (February 12) :324-26.

Gramsci, Antonio. 1973. *Letters from Prison*. Selected, translated, and introduced by Lynne Lawner. New York and London: Harper and Row.

Havens, Murray Clark; Leiden, Carl; and Schmitt, Karl M. 1970. *The Politics of Assassination*. Englewood Cliffs, N.J.: Prentice-Hall.

Hilberg, Raul. 1961. *The Destruction of the European Jews*. Chicago: Quadrangle Books.

———. 1976. *The Role of the German Railroads in the Destruction of the Jews*. Unpublished monograph.

Horowitz, Irving Louis. 1973. *War and Peace in Contemporary Social and Philosophical Theory*. London: Souvenir Press. Originally published 1957. New York: Humanities Publishers.

———. 1975. "Science and Revolution in Contemporary Sociology." *The American Sociologist* 10, no. 2 (May):73-78.

Jones, Margaret, and Ruge, Gero. 1975. "Crime and Punishment in China." *Atlas: World Press Review* 22, no. 9 (September):19-22.

Ledeen, Michael. 1973. "The 'Jewish Question' in Fascist Italy." Paper delivered at the American Historical Association, San Francisco, December 1973. Unpublished.

Lerner, William. 1975. *Statistical Abstract of the United States* (96th Annual Edition). U.S. Department of Commerce. Washington, D.C.: U.S. Government Printing Office.

Levitan, Sar A., and Johnston, William B. 1975. *Indian Giving: Federal Programs for Native Americans*. Baltimore, Md.: The Johns Hopkins University Press.

Lewis, Norman. 1974. "Genocide." *A Documentary Report on the Conditions of Indian Peoples in Brazil*. Berkeley, Calif.: Indigena, and American Friends of Brazil.

Lifton, Robert Jay. 1967. *Death in Life: Survivors of Hiroshima*. New York: Random House.

Martyrs and Heroes Remembrance Authority. 1975. *The Holocaust*. Jerusalem: Vad Vashem.

Mills, C. Wright. 1959. *The Sociological Imagination*. New York: Oxford University Press.

Morgenthau, Henry. 1918. *Ambassador Morgenthau's Story*. New York: Doubleday-Page.

Parsons, Talcott. 1949. *Some Sociological Aspects of the Fascist Movements: Essays on Sociological Theory*. Glencoe, Illinois. The Free Press-Macmillan.

Patterson, William L. 1970. *We Charge Genocide: The Historic Petition to the United Nations for Relief from a Crime of the United States Government against the Negro People*. New York: International Publishers. Originally published 1951. Civil Rights Congress.

———. 1971. *The Man Who Cried Genocide: An Autobiography*. New York: International Publishers.

Pollock, John C. 1975. "Violence, Politics, and Elite Performance: The Political Sociology of *La Violencia* in Colombia." *Studies in Comparative International Development* 10, no. 2 (Summer):22-50.

Reich, Wilhelm. 1970. *The Mass Psychology of Fascism*. Translated by Vincent Carfagno. New York: Farrar, Straus, and Giroux.

Ribeiro, Darcy. 1971. *The Americas and Civilization*. Translated by Linton L. Barrett and Marie Barrett. New York: E. P. Dutton.

Rosenbaum, H. Jon, and Sederberg, Peter C. 1976. *Vigilante Politics*. Philadelphia: The University of Pennsylvania Press.

Rummel, R. J. 1969. "Dimensions of Foreign and Domestic Conflict Behavior: A Review of Empirical Findings." In *Theory and Research on the Causes of War*. Edited by D. G. Pruitt and R. C. Snyder. Englewood Cliffs, N.J.: Prentice-Hall.

Sartre, Jean Paul. 1968. *On Genocide*. Boston: Beacon Press.

Schultheis, Michael. 1975. "The Ugandan Economy and General Amin, 1971-1974." *Studies in Comparative International Development* 10, no. 3 (Fall):3-34.

Seeley, John R. 1963. "Social Science: Some Probative Problems." In *Sociology on Trial*. Edited by Maurice Stein and Arthur Vidich. Englewood Cliffs, N.J.: Prentice-Hall.

Solzhenitsyn, Alexandr I. 1973. *The Gulag Archipelago 1918-1956*. New York and London: Harper and Row.

Spranger, Eduard. 1928. *Types of Men: The Psychology and Ethics of Personality*. Translated by Paul J. W. Pigors. Halle: Niemeyer.

Steiner, John M. 1976. *Power Politics and Social Change in National Socialist Germany*. The Hague: Mouton Publishers.

Stokes, William S. 1971. "Violence as a Power Factor in Latin American Politics." In *Conflict and Violence in Latin American Politics*. Edited by Francisco José Mireno and Barbara Mitrani. New York: Thomas Y. Crowell.

Trimberger, Ellen Kay. 1976. *Revolution from Above: Military Bureaucrats and Development in Japan, Turkey, Egypt, and Peru*. New Brunswick, N.J.: Transaction Books.

United Nations. 1949. *Yearbook of the United Nations, 1947-48*. New York.

United Nations. 1950. *Yearbook of the United Nations, 1948-49*. New York.

Walzer, Michael. 1970. *Obligations: Essays on Disobedience, War, and Citizenship*. New York: Simon and Schuster.

Weisbord, Robert G. 1975. *Genocide? Birth Control and the Black American*. Westport, Connecticut: Greenwood Press.

Wiesel, Elie. 1976. *Messengers of God: Biblical Portraits and Legends*. New York: Random House.

Wilson, Richard W. 1974. *The Moral State: A Study of the Political Socialization of Chinese and American Children*. New York: The Free Press-Macmillan.

Woolf, S. J. 1968. *The Nature of Fascism*. New York. Random House.

Zawodny, J. K. 1962. *Death in the Forest: The Story of the Katyn Forest Massacre*. South Bend, Ind.: University of Notre Dame Press.

Index